Stone and Tree Sh...

An Exploration
of Sacred and Secular Wells
in County Louth

Susan Connolly
Anne-Marie Moroney

Flax Mill Publications
Drogheda Ireland

Flax Mill Publications
34 Ballypark, Flax Mill Lane,
Drogheda, Co. Louth, Ireland.

ISBN Paperback 0 9533822 0 6
ISBN Hardback 0 9533822 1 4

Design & Typesetting
D's Design & Print Centre,
Bettystown, Co. Meath, Ireland.
John Moloney, Greenhills, Drogheda.

Photography
Anne-Marie Moroney and Susan Connolly

Cover Design
Batik by Anne-Marie Moroney

Drawings & Map
Anne-Marie Moroney

This publication has received support from the Heritage Council under the
1998 Publications Grant Scheme.

Printed by
ColourBooks Ltd.
Baldoyle Industrial Estate, Dublin 13, Ireland.

Contents

Foreword - Patricia Lysaght —————————— 1

Introduction ——————————————— 5

Tobercro - Susan Connolly————————————— 6

One
Well Fever - Susan Connolly

Well Fever ————————————————— 11
Toberhullamog, Salterstown ——————————— 14
Saint Dennis's Well, Clogher—————————— 15
Tobar Mháire, Mullary————————————— 16
Saint Feichín's Well, Termonfeckin ——————— 17
Tobar Mhuire, Cappoge ———————————— 18
Toberanelshy, Gallstown ——————————— 19
Garrett's Well, Hacklim ——————————— 20
Toberdoney, Shanlis ————————————— 21
Sunday's Well, Kilcrony———————————— 22
Saint Mobhí's Well, Grange, Skerries——————— 24
Spa Well, Marley————————————— 25
Lady Well, Slane ——————————————— 27
The Stillness of Trees ————————————— 29
Tobar an tSolais, Killineer ——————————— 30

Two
Sunwise Around the Well
A Year's Journey 1996 - Anne-Marie Moroney

Tobar an tSolais, Killineer ——————————— 33
Saint Columcille's Well, Glasallen, County Meath ——— 34
Toberboice Well, Mell————————————— 36
Sally Well, Mell ——————————————— 37
Saint Brigid's Well, Tullyallen ————————— 38
Some Wells in the Tullyallen Area ———————— 38
Wells in Coolfore ——————————————— 40
Wells under Red Mountain ——————————— 41

Well in the Woods of Beaulieu House — 41
Splink Well, near Baltray — 42
Saint Feichín's Well, Termonfeckin — 42
Trinity Well, Termonfeckin — 43
Castle Well, Termonfeckin — 44
Saint Dennis's Well, Clogher — 44
Toberhullamog, Saint Colman's Well, Salterstown — 46
Tobershowney, Carntown — 47
Well at Listoke, Commons — 47
Toberfinn, Fieldstown — 48
The 'Comfortable' Well, Brownstown — 49
Tober Maura, Mullary — 49
Saint Mairéad's Well, Toberdoney House — 50
Saint Finian's Well, Dromin — 51
Saint Patrick's Well, Stickillen — 52
Tobar Mhuire, Cappoge — 53
Saint Brigid's Well, Dunleer — 54
Tobar Mhichíl, Charlestown — 55
Toberanelshy, Gallstown — 55
Spa Well, Marley — 56
Toberdoney, Shanlis — 57
Saint Patrick's Well, Kilpatrick — 58
Garrett's Well, Hacklim — 59
Sunday's Well, Kilcrony — 60
Saint Ronan's Well, Dromiskin — 61
Saint Ultan's Well, Drumgoolan — 61
Saint Patrick's Well, Channonrock — 62
Ladywell, Marshes Upper, Dundalk — 63
Saint Brigid's Well, Faughart Upper — 64
'White' Well, Dowth, County Meath — 66
'Verruca' Well, Fennor, Slane, County Meath — 67
Saint John's Well, Mornington, County Meath — 68
Saint Columcille's Well, Calliaghstown, County Meath — 69
Lady Well, Slane Castle Demesne, County Meath — 69
Saint Mobhí's Well, Grange, near Skerries, County Dublin 71
Saint Brigid's Well, Tobersool, County Dublin — 72
Some Drogheda Wells — 73

Map with Distribution of Wells ————————————— 77

Glossary ————————————————————————— 79

Bibliography ————————————————————— 81

Acknowledgements ————————————————— 85

Sponsors ————————————————————————— 86

Index ————————————————————————————— 87

"Do you hear?' said the little prince. "We have wakened the well, and it is singing ..."

Antoine de Saint-Exupéry

FOREWORD

Chughatsa a thána, a thobair naomhtha
In ainm Dé is na naomh le chéile.
Chughatsa a thána ag insint scéil duit,
Is ar lorg mo leighis i gcúntas Dé ort.

To thee I came, o blessed well,
In the name of God and all the saints.
To thee I came to tell my story,
And to seek a cure on God's account.

All week I had looked forward to visiting Lady Well in the grounds of Slane Castle, Co. Meath. The 15th of August, feastday of the Assumption of Our Lady, is pattern day at the well. In the late evening, young and old were making their way to and from the well, many carrying a bottle of water. Couples, too, strolled along, enjoying the view of the castle and the river Boyne and each other's company. It was a day out, an annual excursion.

At the well, too, people greeted each other warmly. Some withdrew from the well to speak quietly in the background. Others prayed silently by the stream, near a statue of Our Lady standing on a bed of laurel and flowers. Some touched their eyes with water as they blessed themselves, scooped a little clay in a laurel leaf, and then waited for their turn to go down a step into the narrow well to 'Bring home water/on Lady Day'. Nearby, the well-stream poured noisily into the ancient Boyne, meeting sacred water on its race to the sea. And, as the evening closed in, people slowly climbed the steep path between the trees away from the well. In that clearing in the wood by the river Boyne, there was a sense of sanctuary, of water blessed by pilgrim prayers, and ground long hallowed by pilgrim feet.

Lady Well of Slane is one of several thousand wells regarded as 'holy' or 'blessed', which are dotted throughout the landscape of Ireland. It is also one of the wells celebrated in poetry and prose in this delightful book which deals mainly with the wells of the southern part of the county Louth countryside. From this collection we learn that Lady Well of Slane is one of only three wells mentioned in the volume, at which the custom of holding a 'pattern' (Ir. *patrún*, 'patron') or a day of special devotion to mark the feastday of the patron saint, is observed — the other two being Ladywell, Marshes Upper, Dundalk, on the 15th of August, to celebrate Our Lady, and Saint Brigid's Well, Faughart Hill, on the 1st of February, to honour one of the three patron saints of Ireland, Saint Brigid, *Muire na nGael*. People walk *deiseal* or sunwise around Saint Brigid's Well, and on the large laurel bush close by they leave pieces of cloth, threads, rosaries or other personal items, perhaps, in thanksgiving for, or in the hope of receiving, spiritual or physical favours, especially the curing of eye complaints.

Ireland's other two patron saints, Patrick and Columcille, are also remembered in the holy well dedications appearing in this book. But like so many of the wells mentioned here, these wells, too, have been affected by changing times and attitudes. An attempt to inaugurate or, perhaps, revive a pattern at Saint Patrick's Well, Stickillen townland, county Louth, in the 1950s was unsuccessful — just as attempts at the revitalisation of customs or traditions often are when the conditions in which they grew and prospered no longer obtain. The fond recollection included in this book, of Saint Columcille's Well in Collon parish, provides a glimpse of a pattern in its heyday, when the local people decorated the well, when lighted candles flickered in the breeze, and when the older people prayed and did the rounds in their bare feet while the young folk met and mingled and dreamt of the future.

This book includes not only holy wells, however. Mentioned also are wells which provided or provide water for domestic use, and one of the very pleasing aspects of the volume is the authors' sense of discovery of a hidden landscape close to home, during their year's journey in search of these wells. Attention is lavished, in poetry and prose, on geographical location and topography, and 'townland names' dance 'to the sound/of their own word music'. Some of the holy wells, in particular, are in nooks and corners of fields, overgrown and neglected but waiting to be rediscovered, some are still taken care of by local people, while others have been filled in or have been made remote in farms and walled estates. Some others, though 'fragile in old age', are holding their ground, and are still greeted by occasional visitors who come to pray in the hope perhaps of seeing a fish in the well and being granted their request; or to give thanks and leave a token '... threads of red cashmere', nearby. Other holy wells are now in the grounds of private houses, some even in suburbia. The domestic wells still in use are more accessible, such as the well at Listoke (or, 'the well at Ballymakenny'), and the well in the woods of Beaulieu House, while the disused domestic wells of Drogheda are now closed over, or hidden under buildings, most notably the medieval well in Dyer Street which briefly saw the light of day again during excavations in 1996.

Other wells with strong otherworld associations of their own are located in wilder places, in outcrops, mounds, or close by the sea, 'a wave/wedged between/rocks'.

The wells discovered at journey's end, were clearly a surprise and a delight for the authors, and they have sensitively celebrated them in this book. With them we marvel at the careful stonework of the holy wells — the well-linings, steps, and the canopies with niches for statues and vessels for drinking the water of the well. We can imagine Spa Well, Marley townland, with its elaborate structures waiting, like Atlantis, to be rediscovered in a sea of scrub and vegetation which now overwhelms it, or, in more gentle settings, the 'round pool under sloe blossoms', or 'the well nestling in the roots of a stout ash tree'. We can also picture the water in these wells, bubbling up clear, cool and refreshing, and the flora decorating the wells — 'ivy and hart's-tongue nod at the water's edge and flag irises proudly wave their yellow flowers'.

If the presence of a 'huge, powerfully-bent ash tree' (the ash being one of the sacred trees of Ireland), and of 'a battered hawthorn tree', signalling and guarding a well-site, evoke far-flung and ancient associations of the veneration of wells and trees, the presence in the landscape of the other wells (quite distinct from the holy wells) with strong otherworld associations, enforces that impression. In Gallstown townland, there is Toberanelshy, perhaps *Tobar an Aill Sí*, 'Well of the Fairy Cleft', located in a hollow on a bushy slope. In Carnstown townland, there is Tobershowney, with its enduring May morning magical associations, and *Tobar na gCorr*, 'Well of the Herons'(?) in Navan townland, with its legend of the three white water horses coming out of the well at night to graze. Above all, there is Garrett's Well (*Tobar Ghearóid*) in a mound near Garrett's Fort with its cave-like depression, and its associated medieval European messianic tradition of a great sleeping warrior (in Leinster tradition, *Gearóid Iarla*, Gerald, one of the Earls of Kildare) and his ghostly cavalry waiting in a cave or cavern to be awakened by the signal — a beautiful sword that must be drawn fully from its scabbard by a man courageous and strong enough to do so — and thence to issue forth from the mound for the sake of Ireland.

The year's journey in search of wells evoked in this beautiful and unusual book, is an act of remapping aspects of the landscape and personality of county Louth. For many people, still, on the eve of the third millennium, drinking the water of a holy well confers a sense of physical and spiritual well-being.

"I am thirsty for this water," said the little prince. "Give me some of it to drink ... "

Patricia Lysaght
Lá Fhéile Muire sa bhFómhar, 1998

INTRODUCTION

The fieldwork which is the foundation of this book was carried out in 1996. In the course of that year we spent many hours in libraries trying to locate holy wells on the Ordnance Survey Maps. Then, on most Sunday afternoons, weather permitting, we searched for those wells in the landscape. Warm clothes, wellington boots, a walking stick, a torch, and a cup, became part of the equipment essential for our outings.

Altogether, we visited about one hundred wells, sacred and secular, mostly in the southern half of county Louth. Some of these were holy wells. Others were for domestic use, and others still drew us to them because of associated legends. Many local people helped us to find the wells and told us stories about them. The result of those afternoon excursions and research in books, newspapers and maps, is now contained in these pages.

Not all of the wells visited are mentioned here. Susan Connolly wrote poems about those wells that left an impression on her. Anne-Marie Moroney has described the wells which most interested her in terms of healing attributes, setting in nature, accessibility, quality of water and accompanying stories.

Our research shows that many of these wells and the traditions associated with them are on the point of extinction. Strong traditions of patterns and stations are still associated with only three of the wells described. However, many individuals are still visiting some of the other wells and making their devotions privately, as rags, shells, stones and coins left as offerings show. Certain people or families have undertaken to care for a well with which they have a particular affinity.

We hope that this book will encourage other interested people to find wells, sacred or otherwise, to meet the local people, and to discover a landscape which might be unknown to them, for these wells are often situated in remote places which have their own beauty.

Susan Connolly

Anne-Marie Moroney
August 1998

Tobercro

      Our map brings us to Carrick,
to an old woman standing at her gate.
'We're looking for a well near Carrick
Hill. Is that the hill?'
'Yes, that's Carrick, - but there's
no well about that I know of.'
'Isn't there one called Tobercro?'
Her eyes cloud over: 'I used to walk
my children there ...'
'Do you know where it is?'
'Go up Carrick Hill and down, and go
as far again.'
      We come to a rocky field. Two
women direct us further: 'Go along
the quarry road, over the field.
It's by a corner, fenced in.'
      A man says he knows a spring:
'Will I take you there?'

*

Across the field
over a fence,
a rose-shadowed spring

waits for us:
Tobar na Croise Naofa -
'The Well of the Holy Cross'.

Intimacy of a forgotten place!
Neglected and overgrown
the well is beautiful.

As if no one had ever
seen it before

ONE

WELL FEVER

Susan Connolly

for Patricia

Well Fever

1.
Toberboice, Tobereisk,
Tobar na Caillí.
Saint Brigid's Well,
Dunleer -
lost, found
and lost again.
Saint Mairéad's Well,
Toberdoney -
a babbling well.
Garrett's Well, Hacklim;
Garrett's well of the
setting sun

Tobar Sí, Gallstown -
the 'fairy well'.
Spa Well, Marley -
a well that takes care
of itself.
Tobar Mháire, Mullary:
dedicated to Mary -
a spring fragile
in old age.
The well at Listoke -
some call it
the well at Ballymakenny

Shanlis, Hacklim, Cappoge,
Kildemock, Carnanbreaga -
townland names
dancing to the sound
of their own word-music.
Toberfinn, Tobertheorin,
Toberhullamog.
And three more yet
to find -
Tobar mín, Tobar Chomhaill,
Tobar na gCorr,
'well of the herons' ...

2.
Let every step
bring me closer.
I want to taste
your stillness.
An ash tree
is a signpost
to you,
a roadside stile
your threshold.
Motorists
zoom past you
unaware.
I sense
your different
guises.
Always the same
surprise
as I find you,
touch your water
that lets me
see further,
the other
deeper side
of here

Toberhullamog, Salterstown

Only a few steps
from the sea
I found water,
a wave
wedged between
rocks

So fresh and sweet
to taste,
it surprised me,
like waking to
a carpet of moss
over November

Saint Dennis's Well, Clogher

A dark space
beside the old harbour
drew me in

to discover
hart's tongue,
deep-green

and shell-gifts
thumbed between
flat stones.

More alive here,
in this peaceful
cove ...

I saw more
than my reflection
in the water.

Across ditch
and sodden field
I went -

the well by the sea
like a shell
in me

Tobar Mháire, Mullary

Cradled
in the roots
of an ash tree,
forgotten
and neglected -
I'd like
to turn back
the clock,
see you
as you were
when people
believed
in you

Despite
a rusty car-
bonnet thrown
over you,
five steps
deep in mud,
plastic bags
everywhere -
this is still
the perfect
place for
prayer

Saint Feichín's Well, Termonfeckin

Once you stood alone
in a field
in Feichín Valley.
Sheltered now
by a tall, shapely
ash tree,
you dwell in
rural suburbia

This garden's owner
takes good care
of you.
She knows you best.
How your waters
ripple and run
in five streams
underground

Much older
than nearby house
or tree,
I like to think
you look after
the family
growing up
here

for Jackie Tyrrell

Tobar Mhuire, Cappoge

January, - a Sunday,
we came to this field
with a crowbar,

levered up
the heavy flagstone
covering you.

Sunlight poured in.
Our talk a century
of stories

about you.
Down on my belly
I leaned in,

touched
your stonework,
your murky water.

Later
I felt the usual
heaviness

lift from me,
the sight restored
to my inner eye

Toberanelshy, Gallstown

An urge to find
the 'fairy well'
led us here,
then lost us.
Now we search
for each other.
I feel
I am invisible,
have stepped
inside a maze.
Alone among
the thorn trees
and gorse
of Carnanbreaga

Luring me deep
inside their world,
they whisper:
Tobar Sí -
here, here,
over here

Garrett's Well, Hacklim

When the setting sun
entered Garrett's
slit-eyed well

I caught a glimpse
of Hacklim's
heart and soul.

Whoever
finds
the sword

hanging
on a nail inside
the rath -

will free
Gearóid Iarla's
horseback

army, asleep
here
for centuries.

A roar of thunder
from deep inside
the hill -

Hacklim's
galloping
heartbeat

Toberdoney, Shanlis

Near a whitethorn
dressed in rags,
Sunday's Well
is a clear pool
enclosed by
stones

In a rocky nook
beside the tree
I found
a plastic cup.
I sat there
sipping water

My dark mood
broke
like a cloud.
Each thought a raindrop.
Each raindrop
a tiny well

Sunday's Well, Kilcrony

Yellow flowers
my threshold,
'the pass' -
a parting
in the grass,
'the noisy tree' -
an aspen.
A white rag
knotted
to a thorn,
threads of red
cashmere.
The steep climb
down
discloses
my well-house,
dry bed of withered
ash leaves

Few visit me.
But since
Peggy Martin
brought you here,
I have been
happy.
She told
how as a girl
she and her friends
played games
around me.
I gave them
drinks of water

Like a small child
I listened
to her story.
Like a mother
listening
to her grown up
daughter

Saint Mobhí's Well, Grange, Skerries

Sycamore
tree
or
guardian
spirit?

Well-house
of huge
rocks
raised high
above
water
trickling
since
the
first dawn

Spa Well, Marley

Slashing my way
through nettle,
thistle, thorn

I open up
the path to you,
am surprised

to find you
brimming
with clear water.

At the same time
you open up
a path in me.

Finding you
is to find words
I need to say.

Outside his lodge
a man points
the way:

'Go up the road
as far as you can see
from here. Turn left

where the sun stops,
and cross
two cornfields.'

Under a clear blue sky
his words lead
to you

Lady Well, Slane

WATER CLAY LAUREL WATER CLAY LAUREL WATER CLAY Lady Well LAUREL CLAY WATER

The castle gates
open,
the old path
busy all day.
People talk,
people pray.
Flower-shrine.
Amber river.
I break off
a sprig of laurel,
scoop up clay.
I dip an empty
bottle
in the well.
Bring home water
on Lady Day

Lady Well, Slane
August 15th

The Stillness of Trees

Here, in this wilderness,
we learn
the stillness of trees.

From a high branch a bird
welcomes us:
'Forget the world!'

A strong, silent
presence ...
It must be the trees.

I'd love to be like them,
birdsong haunting
my branches.

My spirits brighten.
Strong, silent trees
watch us leave.

And that high, hypnotic
voice calls out:
'Goodnight!'

at Saint Mairéad's Well, Toberdoney

Tobar an tSolais, Killineer

When the well
of light
is bloodied,
and the way lost,
I want to be
like that ash;
at midnight
to uproot myself,
and lead my life
elsewhere

But when words
well up in me
like tears,
I'll know
I have found
my way

for Anne-Marie

TWO

Sunwise Around the Well

A Year's Journey 1996

Anne-Marie Moroney

for Tony

*with thanks for his
patience and understanding*

Tobar an tSolais,
Killineer Townland

This 'Well of the Light' is an enchanting place to visit during the summer months. (Permission should be obtained from Mr. Eamon Briscoe). The well-site is less than half a mile distant from the reservoir at Barnattin, just east of the little stream.

The spring is very strong, and despite several clay drainage pipes, it still swamps the area, where very old and also younger trees form a copse. One huge, powerfully-bent ash tree, guards the site, and a battered hawthorn tree, heavy with old age, leans protectively over a damp area that might have contained the well. The moisture welling up produces lush, bright green grass.

But the well was not always where it is now, according to an old story. An 18th-century legend tells of a local butcher, Paddy Sloan, who, despite repeated warnings, polluted the well by washing the entrails of animals in the water. One night the well, accompanied by a huge ash tree with hundreds of lighted candles on it, was seen to move through the air, from Balgatheran Townland in Mellifont Parish, across the little stream to Killineer Townland, where it settled. The late Miss Kathleen Pentony, born in 1900, recalled neighbours whose daughter had witnessed this event. The butcher, stricken by an infirmity, was unable to continue with his work.

The name of this well might be derived from the candles that lit the way for the moving well, but on a good day in summer, in the sun and dappled shade at the well, one can see the light dance and move in the breeze.

It is good to take a little time at this 'well', to enjoy the light, think of the legend and taste its water. Unfortunately, the mug that used to be kept at this holy well is no longer there. The water was said to cure many ailments, including sore eyes, and people used to leave offerings at the well.

Despite the drought in 1995, the well continued to give its water, much to the relief of the thirsty cattle.

Saint Columcille's Well,
Collon Parish, Glasallen Townland, County Meath

'When this well was closed over it rose again in the kitchen of the Tower House,' according to many local residents.

The present owner of the land, Mr. Sonny Halpenny, told us that, unknown to his family, a developer filled in the well in 1965 and removed the hedge and bushes around it.

Saint Columcille's Holy Well was an important place of pilgrimage for many centuries. The pattern commenced on the 9th of June, the saint's feastday, and continued until the 18th of June. Priests led pilgrimages from Collon to the well on the Sunday during the pattern. 'Many people,' said the late Mrs. L. Carton, 'walked across the sometimes very muddy fields to reach the well.' It was set in a sloping field west of Hurcle Hill and north of the Doagh stream. Most pilgrims used one of three routes: some came down the lane to Cunningham's house, then through fields and over a plank into the well-field; others came from 'Elliot's' house on the Hurcle Road west, while still others crossed from the Slane road between Glasallen and White Cross east through fields.

Isaac Butler wrote in 1744: 'The Well of Cullumcille to the west of Mellifont has good water, very pure and lathers pretty soon, there is a great Patron kept on the 9th of June, several thousands of the country people meet here who have solemn service performed in different parcels and by several priests, after which they eat, drink, are merry, and dance and play football, sometimes great quarrels arise and several goe home with broken and sore limbs.'

Mrs. Simpson, Ardagh Lane, told us that everyone went to the well on pattern day. The field used to be crowded with people enjoying themselves, and there was no fighting or drinking. It used to be a private pilgrimage and a pleasant outing to this big well with good, ice-cold water.

Flag stones led down to the well and another smooth flag covered it. One had to bend down to get to the water. Mrs. Sheila Tiernan, née Cunningham, remembers that flowers were placed behind the well; her brothers used to clean it out each year for the pattern and her family provided a mug. People would drink the water, wash their faces and hands with it and would carry it home in large bottles. Nancy McGrane recalls that the spring was very strong and that it drained into a stream. The late Mrs. Frances Barnett remembered mostly the candles that were lit at the well. Bunches of flowers were tied to the bushes. Rags, string, ribbons and garters were hung on the branches; some pilgrims wore a similar string around their socks also. Everyone, even men, walked around the well in their bare feet, saying the rosary. Five posts in the fence around the well represented a decade of the rosary apiece. Some people did the rounds three times, thus saying saying all fifteen decades.

The well was said to cure many ailments, including backache and eye disorders. The water was also used to protect the house and its occupants, especially during thunderstorms. Everyone loved coming to Saint Columcille's Well: young people watched the devotions performed by others from the high ground or rolled down the slope for fun. Girls were allowed out on that day, away from the watchful eye of their parents and young men came to admire them, according to Mr. Peter McDonnell.

Today, the easiest route to the well-field is from the Hurcle road. The site of the well, although now covered over, is in the steep part, at the western edge of the field, where the boundary is shaped like an 'elbow'. The spring, which can be detected with a dowsing rod, is very strong. Some of the water flows into a clay pipe and drains into a gripe where it may be collected - it is cool and tastes good. This is a chalybeate well (containing iron); when the outflow is left undisturbed for a time, a bright red deposit forms at the opening of the pipe. The rest of the water flows down the hill saturating the ground and then drains into the stream.

Will this well and its water ever see the sun again? Although closed for over thirty years the memories of this well are very strong in the minds of the people.

Toberboice Well, Mell Townland

The way to Buithe's Well is from Mell in Drogheda down Toberboice Lane to the small industrial estate. Many years ago Toberboice Cottage, a house with a nice garden and orchard, and other houses and cabins, formed a small community there. The water from the well behind Toberboice Cottage was used by the residents. Nuala Coleman (née Collins) grew up in the area. According to her a level in the garden wall regulated the flow of the well-water. The spring was very strong. Sometimes the lane seemed to want to lift off because of the pressure of the water underneath. The water was piped to the Linen Hall and it supplied Casey Connolly's Brewery through wooden pipes, as well as Preston's Distillery and Cairnes's Brewery.

Today, the water from the former well gushes from two clay pipes into a pool on the southern side of the industrial site. The clean water is collected by Mell residents for drinking and tea-making. A large boulder by the well, when warmed by the sun, is a good place to take a rest and to listen to the relaxing sound of running water.

Toberboice, as old stories from Mell tell us, was formed by Saint Buithe, who was born there. When his father wanted to have him baptised only seawater was available. Two monks, who were passing in a boat on the Boyne, pressed the infant's finger into the ground and a spring gushed out.

Across the reeds is the River Boyne into which the well drains. Along the Ramparts Walk on the southern side of the river, several springs course down the slope, one of them ending in a well that contains a grate. This might have been called **Dawes Well**, after an old Drogheda family, one of whose members was Mayor of Drogheda in 1470.

Cains Well in Mell, outside Fountain House and Cottages, used to be popular because of its good quality water. The big stone structure and the steps were a favourite gathering place for the young and the courting couples. It was closed in 1955 and a manhole now covers it.

Sally Well

The Sally (or Sallow) Well is in the north-west of Mell Townland. It is in a corner of a field belonging to Mr. N. Carolan, on the left side of the road going up the Hill of Rath. A gap in the thorny hedge and a stout plank across the drain help one into the field. The well is enclosed by a rectangular cut-stone structure, backed with rough stones and earth and covered with two heavy stone slabs. Another slab holds the water in, but over time the whole structure has sagged and spread out gently. The water seeps through the stonework to form a pool, much used by the grazing cattle. Do not confuse this well with *Tobar an tSolais* which lies in a nearby townland.

Saint Brigid's Well / *Tobar Domhnaigh* (Sunday's Well), Tullyallen

Only the older people of the small village of Tullyallen remember this well and recall drinking water from it after Mass on Sundays, or before going to school. Saint Brigid's Well is close to the main road where the cars flash past. Ferns, dead leaves, mud and many successive layers of tarmacadam on the lane, are closing up the well which is on the eastern side of the Old School Lane. The well is lined with stones and a strong slab protects the water.

A previous owner of the house, in the bank of whose garden the well is sunk, decided to fill the well with stones, as children used to play there. During the night, while asleep, he is said to have heard strange rumbling noises, as if stones were being moved around. He took it as a sign that filling in the well was wrong and on the following day opened it up again.

Saint Brigid's Well, like many wells named after this saint, is said to have a cure for eye diseases. Mrs. Eileen Murphy told us of a man who got hot ashes into his eyes one Sunday. He was told to go to the well and to wash his eyes in the holy water. The man was cured and was then able to work the whole Sunday after that!

It is hoped that a planned village renewal programme for Tullyallen will deal with the well in a fitting manner.

Some Wells in the Tullyallen Area

The families in the three houses in **King William's Glen** between

Tullyallen and Oldbridge used to get water from a well in the woods.

Eagerly helped by the children of the Johnson family who live in one of the houses, we followed the 'pass' to this well across the small stream that runs through the Glen. On the other side the path became hidden under the fallen leaves of the huge mature trees growing in the Glen. The late Mrs. Carton, who lived in the oldest house there, said that her children used to play music sitting in the branches of those trees!

The rectangular well, which looks a little like an outdoor fireplace, is under an old and a young beech tree. Built of stone and red brick, it is still about 60cm deep. Children, and sometimes a lucky tourist camping in the shelter of those beautiful trees, enjoy its quiet presence.

On the **Townley Hall Road**, beside Gibney's house, is a large roomy well built into the roadside bank. John Pentony used to keep it clean and now the Gibney family look after it. The angular and sharp-edged stones enclosing the well are in many shades of grey, blue, red and green while the lintel is quite straight and plain. The well is still in good repair, its water unaffected by drought and much appreciated by the local community during a dry summer.

Near the former sawmill, on the northern edge of the woods in **Townley Hall**, a little-used avenue leads towards the big house. The Murphy family used to walk this way and then along the small path beside the stone-lined stream to the big rectangular structure of red brick, fringed with ivy and ferns. Its cold water is so clear that it can hardly be seen and is deeply shaded by old, tall pine trees.

The well at **Oldbridge** is often noticed by people as they pass by on the busy road from Slane to Drogheda. It is situated outside the house of the late Dr. A. Hoey and Mrs. Hoey. The modern roadside wall incorporates the well which may be approached from the road, and there are also steps on either side leading into the garden of the house. The inscription over the well reads: 'Holy Well, D'Alton Historian'. The D'Alton in question was the author of a history of Drogheda.

Wells in Coolfore, Begrath and Coolfore Townlands

There are a good many domestic wells still to be seen in the townlands of Begrath and Coolfore, as piped water became available to the houses there only in the 1960s as a result of a private water scheme.

Beyond an old chapel site dating from the Penal times, in the parish of Mellifont, is a well in a hedge - a round pool under sloe blossoms, now completely forgotten. It is not known if this was a holy well. During Penal times people used to gather at this chapel and tree for Mass when a priest was able to be present. Priests were hidden in several places in the area during times of persecution.

Five wells in Coolfore were 'Erected by William Drummond Delap Esq., June 1860 and 1861' for the people of the area, as the inscriptions on the cut-stone well-houses read. Situated along the roads on top of the hill, most of them are still filled with water. The steps leading down to one of the wells are so narrow that it must have been difficult for an adult to get water from this well.

Along a lane past O'Grady's Gardens, in land once owned by the late Mary Kate Downey, is a well covered over by a fallen hawthorn tree which is heavily weighed down by ivy. Shallow steps lead down to this well which holds water in summer.

Wells under Red Mountain, Killineer Townland

Two wells are located on the northern side of Carney's Lane, the road which leads from the main road north of Drogheda to the reservoir at Barnattin.

One of the wells, situated in the road verge, is nearly always hidden by the tall grass, but its water is still used at times for drinking.

The other well is located in a field, situated along the bend of the road - a surprise waiting to be discovered just inside the field. It is quite a small well, built with stone slabs, and a mound of earth and a scraggy hawthorn tree shelter it. The primroses along the bank 'dress' this well in spring. Its waters are piped under the road to flow downhill.

Well in the Woods of Beaulieu House, Beaulieu Townland

In the grounds of this house, past the gardens and lawns, close to the River Boyne, a path leads to a well in the woods. We visited the well there with the kind permission of the present owner of Beaulieu House, Mrs. Waddington. Beaulieu House is an unfortified gentleman's residence built between 1660-1666.

The well is tucked away from the path, with a forest of large fern leaves, ivy and hart's-tongue decorating it. Stone steps lead down to the well which has a plentiful and dependable supply of clean, cool water. The circular well-house built with big stones is spacious; a stout stone-stop prevents rainwater, mud and dead leaves from polluting the well.

It is not a forgotten well as it regularly provides excellent drinking water for the residents of Beaulieu House.

Splink Well, Beaulieu Townland

A stretch of road between Queensborough and the bridge at Baltray is lined on one side by a wall. The other side is open to the Boyne estuary.

The smooth curve of the wall suddenly gives way to a deep U-shape, and people speeding past might well wonder why. When you take a few moments to investigate this deep indentation in the wall you will discover the Splink Well, *Tobar na Splince* (the well of the cliff or pinnacle).

Several small arches lead to the well, which is lined with hart's-tongue and moss. It is like a miniature world, with cold, clear water.

Saint Feichín's Well, Termonfeckin

This holy well is on the northern side of the Ballywater river, on the road to Seapoint, in the garden of a private house belonging to Jackie Tyrrell. Access to this beautifully-kept well, situated under a huge, 250-year old ash tree, is through a small gate in the wall.

Nearby, the ruins of Saint Feichín's monastery, the former *tearmann* area (sanctuary) represented by the present-day cemetery and the high crosses, signal the former importance of this site.

The Louth Ordnance Survey Letter of 1835-36, state that: 'Feighen's Well, called by the people *Tobar Feichín* ... it is a shed built of stones covered with green sods as a defence against the summer's sun and the winter's storm; its waters are contained in a metal pan, around which is a circular stone-work raised a few inches above the ground.'

Saint Feichín's feastday is on the 20th of January; but the tradition of stations at the well ceased around 1820. From then on the water was used for domestic purposes.

Tobar Feichín, or the 'Pan Well', has a circular depression at the bottom. Now lined with stones, the well is open at the top and fringed with low bushes. Steps lead down to the clear water. At times tiny duckweed plants make swirling patterns on the water.

Trinity Well,
Termonfeckin

Trinity Well is on the southern bank of the Ballywater stream that winds its way towards the sea. It is to the left of the road, behind the Catholic Church, that leads to the I.C.A. College 'An Grianán'. The well is set into the steep part of the slope, protected by magnificent trees.

The well-house is built of mortared stone and some red bricks with a stone cross on the pointed 'gable'. The water is lined with soft green vegetation on the inside of the well structure, and in autumn the Himalayan Balsam plants that abound at the well, spread their seeds by exploding the pods when touched, giving them their other name of 'Jumping Jack'.

The pattern at this well used to be held on Trinity Sunday (end of May or beginning of June) and the last organised pattern was in 1933. Mrs. Cathleen Carroll remembered that the well used to be dressed with arches and flowers. People blessed themselves while walking on the slippery stones under the arches and drank three sips of the water from a tin mug. Others sat on the hill and chatted to old friends.

Castle Well, Termonfeckin

The lane north of the castle (a tower house) leads on soft green grass down to an area surrounded by bushes and trees. The well is on the boundary wall belonging to the neighbouring house and the overflow runs under lush green vegetation into the next field.

Today, the well supplies water through a hose. A strong wall surrounds and protects it, flags set into the stones provide easy access. The well is at the bottom of the structure, level with the ground. A huge, long stone set into the slope acts as a lintel.

This lovely area hidden behind the castle provides a quiet resting place beside the well, which is still in use, with the help of modern technology.

Saint Dennis's Well, Clogher Townland

A lane in the northern part of Clogherhead village leads to a gate which opens into a deserted farmstead and then continues along an old boreen north to the old harbour in the Fethis.

This harbour is shaped like a deep horseshoe. Stones, polished smooth by the sea, are set into the pale sand like rounded animal shapes. A huge boulder near the water's edge has curved sides, a cleft in the middle, and a water-filled depression on one side.

'Saint Dennis's Gale', which occurs about the time of the saint's feastday, is an east wind that brings herring into the sea around Clogherhead. According to the legend, this wind blew the big stone with the body of the dead saint into the harbour.

The feastday of St. Dennis is on the 29th of September or the 9th of October. In times past there was an extended pattern which might have incorporated both dates; it is possible that other saints were also venerated at this well. On the last day of the pattern, known as 'Sheela's Monday', the 'Mayor' of the area was paraded in ridiculous guise to the well where he was immersed. This custom came to an abrupt end when the last incumbent candidate nearly drowned!

Saint Dennis's Well is set into a bush-covered slope that rises up from the sea. The well is in a tall rectangular structure and only contains water in winter. The large slab covering the well has initials and crosses carefully carved on the hard stone. Were these petitions or marks of gratitude?

In the last century a sailor who lost a leg in an accident at sea is said to have had it re-attached after making a pattern at the well.

The view from the old harbour across Dundalk Bay to the Cooley Mountains is splendid, an ideal place for solitude or good conversation.

Toberhullamog, *(Tobar Cholmóig),*
Saint Colman's Well,
Salterstown, Togher Parish

What a surprise to find this well close to the rolling waves beside the rocks at Salterstown. People enjoying a picnic sitting on the wooden seats do not realise that Saint Colman's Well is near a track that leads to the stony beach. A plaque over the well reads; *'A Cholmóig Naomhtha Guidh Orainn'* ('Saint Colman pray for us') *'Tobar Cholmóig 1913'* ('Saint Colman's Well 1913'). A hollow lined with big round stones, the well contains fresh water. Winter storms and easterly gales throw sand, shells and stones into it and sometimes bury it deeply. Each spring, Mr. John Sarsfield of Annagassan cleans it out and takes care of it during the summer. He collects coins that are dropped into the well and lights candles for the intentions of the visitors to the well. Stones and shells are left as offerings too.

Up to a century ago, an annual pattern took place at the well on the 7th of June, the feast of Saint Colman. The well was visited and from there a procession went to Salterstown church and graveyard. Saint Colman is thought to have been the abbot of the Linn Duachaill monastery at Annagassan.

The well is still visited for eye ailments. Two cures were reported recently, and in older days the water was said to cure the ague (a malarial fever) and other diseases.

Toberhullamog is a special place. Leaving the well and walking on the beach over the rocks, carved and polished by the waves, while looking across the sea to the Cooley Peninsula, is a lovely experience. The metal 'horns' firmly attached to rocks near the water's edge, formerly held up a diving board! A concrete ledge used to have a timber structure over it and served as the ladies' bathing hut. The men had a similar facility south of the 'pier'.

Tobershowney,
Carntown Townland

This important well used to be on the eastern side of the Ballymakenny Road and south of Norris's Mill. During hedge clearing and land development it was covered over.

In the past patterns were held at this well and the water was reputed to have cures.

People also used to go to Tobershowney on May morning as this was said to bring luck, especially for the first person to draw water from it. One young man had been that lucky person repeatedly. But when he returned to the well very early on the following May morning, he was surprised by other youths who jumped out of the bushes where they had spent the night - to be even earlier!

Well At Listoke,
Commons Townland

On the western side of the road between Drogheda and Ballymakenny, just before the gate lodge at Listoke, a beautiful well is tucked away in its own world right under the road.

Big stone steps and a sturdy handrail lead down into this tiny glade beside the road, between shrubs and trees that border the field. At the bottom runs a very small stream; one step is enough to reach the other side.

The well is on the left side, in a fine stone structure built over the cool, clear water; insects called pond skaters enjoy the tranquility of the green and shady place.

People travel from Drogheda with containers to bring some of this good quality water home; the well is kept clean by the people who live in the cottage nearby.

Toberfinn, Fieldstown Townland

North of Fieldstown, down a slope towards Brownstown, is Toberfinn, a well in a quiet piece of ground beside the road, surrounded by grass and shaded by shrubs and thorn trees. A gap in the bank and five steps lead to a stone-lined well filled with cold, clear water. In earlier days a mug was left at the well so that people could drink from it after attending Mass. A deeper outlet and a groove in the top flag drain the well. The water forms a stream which joins Flynn's river.

Toberfinn means 'bright' or 'limpid' well. The well might also be called after Fionn MacCumhaill. An old story explains that he created this well when he took a rock out of the ground and threw it towards Piperstown Townland, where it can now be seen as a standing stone in Culfionn.

Another well, a little way to the north of Toberfinn and on the left side of the road, is in a depression in a field. It is covered with slabs of stone and is used by cattle.

A third well, now safely contained in a concrete structure with a rusty gate, beside the first house in Brownstown, still shows the original rough stone slabs of the well that served the house.

Visiting Toberfinn in January was a bone-chilling experience, but in brighter, warmer weather it is a lovely place for moments of contemplation.

The 'Comfortable' Well, Brownstown Townland

On the Harestown road, close to houses near Fieldstown's new Primary School, is a well built of flat stones and a large slab, situated under the stone wall bordering the road. The grass verge is kept neatly mowed and the well may easily be seen from the road.

The well is in good repair. Large stones protrude on either side of the opening. Were these seats, or were they used for resting the water bucket on them?

A friendly collie dog finds this well very handy and often drinks out of it.

Tober Maura, *Tobar Mháire* (Mary's Well), Mullary

Mullary (pronounced 'Mulléra') is on a crossroad on the 'old main road', south of Dunleer. The ruined church on the small hill originally belonged to the Knights Templars and Hospitallers and later served the Church of Ireland. A lovely, well-cared for graveyard, shaded by mature linden trees, is a peaceful resting place for both Catholics and Protestants.

Tober Maura, at the bottom of the hill and close to the millstream, nestles in the roots of a stout ash. This very old tree bears the scorch marks of candles placed on it by people visiting the well. Flat stones set into the steep slope on either side of the tree helped visitors to reach the well. Finally, three stone steps lead down to the well, a small and quiet pool.

These days the well is hidden under an old car fender to prevent cattle from getting into the hollow under the tree. But one can picture the visitors of long ago making their way down to the well and up again on the other side; one can hear their feet, their prayers and see the candles flicker in the wind.

Saint Mairéad's Well, in the grounds of Toberdoney House, Toberdoney Townland

Toberdoney House may be approached from the road which runs from Dromin to Ardee. A small lane links this road with a parallel road farther north. After passing the house, and an avenue lined with snowdrops in early spring, the well is in a grassy area under a big ash tree, the descendant, probably, of an even older tree. The well is best visited during the dormant season, before the grass, the nettles and other vigorous weeds take over.

The beehive-type structure forming a well-house in the roots of the tree is open at the front where a large stone slab forms part of a water-stop. An inscription on this stone may be seen by bending down into the well. There the letters SH OC 1788 and TH 1700 are engraved.

No specific cures are now attributed to the well, though traditions of pieces of cloth tied to the branches near the well in the early part of this century, might indicate that people came in search of healing. The holding of a pattern at the well is also long ago since a thing of the past, though in the early nineteenth century large crowds are said to have attended on the feast day of the patron saint, when a variety of sporting events took place.

It is interesting to note that in the early nineteenth century the well is called 'The Lord's Well' or 'Sunday Well', titles probably deriving from the Irish name *Tobar Domhnaigh* 'Sunday's Well', the 'Lord's Well'. The name Toberdoney is possibly an earlier designation for the well as the term is found attached to an early settlement form, a fort or *lios*, in Toberdoney townland - *Lios Thobar Domhnaigh* / 'The Fort of Sunday's Well', and the townland of Toberdoney itself, as well as Toberdoney House, obviously bear this name. It would appear that the well was an important focal point in the townland, as there was once a hedge school nearby.

Even today it is possible to imagine the people of long ago walking around this well, praying and drawing the clear water. The well still invites one to do the same. On a sunny day it is a pleasant experience to rest in the grass near the small stream sheltered by bushes and tall trees. Walking over fragrant mint to discover the orchids and flag irises in the *srath* (low lying land beside a river) lets one forget the busy world close by.

Saint Finian's Well, Dromin

Dromin, on the road between Dunleer and Ardee, is where Saint Finian of Movilla settled, founding a monastery there early in the 6th century. 'Saint Finian's Psalter' was written there and when Saint Columcille saw this magnificent manuscript he decided to copy it in secret. It is said that light shone from his fingers to enable him to copy the book at night. This copy caused a war and a great battle was fought at Cooldrumman (*Cuildremne*), County Sligo. After the battle Columcille was forced to leave his native Ireland and settle in Iona.

A road leads north between the present parish church on the left hand and the graveyard on the right side to McCabe's house. Two wells, one holy and the other for domestic use, shaded by thorn trees and strongly defended by brambles, are situated in their garden. Please ask for permission to visit them. Pick a warm day and wear thorn proof clothes and wellington boots for this visit!

The holy well, dedicated to Saint Finian, is 5-6 feet wide. A stone wall, lower at the front to make access easier, encompasses the well. This well is very deep, with good, clear water. Many years ago it was cleaned out by members of the family to see if there was any truth in the old legend that ancient treasures were stored there. Nothing was found ...

Saint Finian's Holy Well used to be visited by people before they emigrated, to pray for a return to Ireland in years to come.

The domestic well, immediately left of the holy well, is smaller, round in shape and lined with stones, and is usually covered with a sheet of metal. The water was formerly used to supply the McCabe household and made excellent tea.

Saint Patrick's Well, Stickillen Townland

On the road from Richardstown Castle to Ardee a signpost points north into a field to Stickillen, *Tigh Chillín* ('Killian's House'). Ruins of a church from the 12th century, a small graveyard and souterrains, mark a former important site. This 'House of Killian' was probably founded in the early Christian period and dedicated to Saint Killian.

In a meadow, about 100 metres southeast of the church, is the site of the former *Tobar Phádraig*. In winter the place is easy to spot: stones, old tree stumps, their roots studded with stones from the former well, bits of fencing posts and barbed wire, are the decaying witnesses to a once well-visited site. In summer nettles grow plentifully among the stones.

There is still a very strong spring under the ground, maybe waiting to be re-opened?

At one time this well was called Saint Brigid's Well. A pattern was inaugurated there in 1956, but eventually the well was closed over.

Now only the older people in the area remember the patterns held on 27th of May, the feast of Saint Killian, to *Tobar Phádraig* and its good, cool water.

Tobar Mhuire, Cappoge Townland, Dunleer Parish

At Cappoge, in a field close to the home of the Callaghan family, is Saint Mary's Well, dedicated to the Blessed Virgin.

The well is now protected by a very heavy concrete slab. When this is lifted, a circular stone-lined well is revealed, the water bubbling up from beneath a stone. A few years ago Veronica and Michael Clerkin cleaned it out with their bare hands.

It is occasionally opened for people who want to pray there, especially around the feast of the Assumption of the Virgin Mary on the 15th of August. The water in this well is said to rise up on the eve of the feastday. It is thought to be especially potent then and is collected by people.

A very large pattern used to take place here. Formerly the well was marked by a lone tree and surrounded by bushes. The lane leading to this field used to be filled with traps and sidecars as whole families came to the well. The rosary was said while doing the rounds of the well, and water was taken from it and carried home.

An old story tells about children who got water from the holy well instead of a domestic well. This water turned to blood when it was boiled in the kettle.

Today, the local people go to visit the well on the evening of the 14th of August. If the slab is not lifted, the water is collected in the gripe, where the well-water runs down the slope, even in a dry season.

Saint Brigid's Well, Dunleer Townland and Parish

Where is, or was, Saint Brigid's Well? In a private garden between the White River and the railway station; on the eastern bank of the White River, now cleaned up by the Office of Public Works, or in an entirely different place, as suggested by Mr. Patsy Mulroy? For an engrossing account of a search organised by Fr. McKeown in 1911 to discover Saint Brigid's Well, the article by Michael Coyle in the County Louth Archaeological and Historical Journal 1954 may be read.

The legend tells of Saint Brigid, who, pursued by a suitor (or a ruffian) realised that her beauty attracted men. As she wanted to remain unmarried, she disfigured herself by plucking out an eye. In Dunleer she bathed her eye in the holy well and had her sight restored miraculously.

The well remained a place of pilgrimage for many centuries and, like many other wells dedicated to Saint Brigid, it was visited by people with eye problems.

Tobar Mhichíl,
Charlestown Townland and Parish

Charlestown, one and a half miles northwest of Ardee, is easily found, as the Church of Ireland spire acts as a guide. On the opposite side of the road is a much older church, now in ruins, surrounded by a graveyard. This church was dedicated to Saint Michael the Archangel, patron saint of the parish.

The well, which is named after the saint, is found in the south-eastern corner of the graveyard, built into the outside of the wall. A big loose slab covers the upright opening. Kneeling down one sees the lovely stonework of the roof and the deep, circular well.

Saint Michael's Well used to be visited by people suffering from stomach ailments. The sick person or a friend sat at the well with a lighted candle, praying and sipping the water for one hour. Apparently the well fell into disuse because of a bad act committed there.

It is a beautifully-kept well and is still used at times. A light is needed to look down into the well and a bottle or small container on a string to bring up some of its excellent water. Some drops of water might trickle down your neck on a rainy day, or you might see them form intersecting circles as they touch the well-water.

Toberanelshy,
Gallstown Townland

The 'fairy well', is that the meaning of the name? The first excursion to find this remote well left a family wandering around in rugged fields, full of small rock outcroppings, bushes and clumps of vegetation, all looking very much alike. Had the fairies led them astray?

The well is best approached from the road that runs past the entrance to Dunleer Quarry and Gallstown House. Shortly afterwards a lane leads south into green fields, dotted with yellow gorse and lacy white blackthorn. Where the lane ends the stone wall acts as a guide to a corner in the wall, a short distance before the southern boundary of the townland. Toberanelshy is not far distant to the east of this corner, situated on a slope, in a hollow and shaded by bushes. This marshy spring, which contains slimy water under a mound of green vegetation, drains into a pond north of it. However, the water tastes fresh and good.

Another explanation of the name of this well is that it might refer to skin ailments. *Tobar an ailsigh*: The well of the sufferers of skin disease. Does this water contain healing substances that helped people in the old days with their skin problems?

Tobertheorin (*Tobar Teorann*) lies in the south-eastern corner of the same townland. The 'Well of the Boundary' is in a very wet area and is difficult to identify.

Spa Well / Saint Brigid's Well, Marley Townland, Marlestown Civil Parish

South of the railway line and the road which runs between Grangebellew and Dunleer, a lane leads over a small bridge and past a lodge. There one has a good view of Rokeby Hall, built by Lord Rokeby, Archbishop of Armagh and Primate of Ireland in the late 18th century.

From the lane where 'the sun stops and the dark trees begin' tracks made by tractors lead through two large wheatfields and past the ruins of the old mortuary chapel. The well is at the southern tip of the Spa Wood.

In all seasons it is difficult to gain access to this well. Even the sparser winter vegetation of briars and bushes defends the well, which is also watched over by a tall service tree.

In former times steps and an arch led down to the water. Walls were erected, about six feet high, to provide shelter for the well and its visiors. On one side the well is set very low and deep into a wall. It is so deeply recessed that even a long walking stick did not touch the end of the chamber. The water is clear, cool, and so plentiful that it spills over towards the surrounding walls.

Nowadays nobody seems to know why it is called the Spa Well. Did the water contain special minerals? Its other name *Tobar Bhríde* (Saint Brigid's Well) points to a probable earlier dedication to that saint. Stations were regularly held there a long time ago.

Unfortunately, during a visit in 1998, this well was found to be much disturbed and inaccessible, as debris from land clearing work had been deposited over it.

Toberdoney (*Tobar Domhnaigh* / Sunday's Well), Shanlis Townland, Ardee

In former times people went to Toberdoney from an old church and graveyard, a walk for fit people! Today, with permission from the McKeever family at Shanlis House south-east of Ardee, a short half-hour walk through their garden and four fields leads to a low lying area where different boundaries meet.

The well rests on a slope, sheltered by several trees with bent and angled branches. Down the slope from the well, water completely covered with bright green vegetation drains away. The rickety plank promising easy access into the next field could quickly give way and topple one into a green bath! So, caution is necessary.

A lovely well, this oval pool is lined with moss-covered stones. Ivy and hart's-tongue nod at the water's edge and the flag irises proudly wave their yellow flowers.

The crystal clear water bubbles up through the sediment in mosaic patterns. Mrs. McKeever regularly leaves a supply of clean plastic cups for people who want to drink the water, which is said to cure asthma.

Rags and rosary beads hanging on the gnarled branches over the well show that this is not a forgotten place. People still come to pray hoping that their problems and illnesses will fade away along with the rags left on the bushes.

But this well does not take kindly to being interfered with: One day a little boy is said to have piddled into its water; the next moment clouds gathered and a thunderclap terrified the offender ...

Saint Patrick's Well, Kilpatrick Townland, Kildemock Parish

This holy well lies in a field north of the home and farm of the Boylan family. Mr. and Mrs. Boylan kindly share their knowledge of the area, and of the well, with visitors and direct them to the well, in the knowledge that they will respect the crops growing in the fields at the time of a visit.

Originally this well was in a different spot. But after it was defiled it closed, and then rose up again in another place in a corner of a field, backed by shrubs and trees. The boys of the neighbourhood carried a large stone from the former site and placed it beside the well.

This stone is said to show (and, indeed the marks are very clear),

Tobar Mhichíl
Charlestown

Toberhullamog
Salterstown

Saint Mairéad's Well
Toberdoney

**Ash tree at Saint
Feichín's Well**
Termonfeckin

Saint Feichín's Well
Termonfeckin

Toberdoney
Shanlis

Saint Patrick's Well
Channonrock

Anne-Marie Moroney at **Toberboice**
Mell

Garrett's Well
Hacklim

Roches Well
Moneymore, Drogheda

Ladywell
Marshes Upper, Dundalk

The 'Comfortable' Well
Susan Connolly at Brownstown

Tobar Mhuire
Cappoge

Well in the Woods
Beaulieu House

Well at Listoke
Ballymakenny Road, Commons Townland

12th Century Well
Dyer Street, Drogheda

Saint Columcille's Well
Calliaghstown, Co. Meath

Saint Mobhí's Well
Grange, near Skerries,
Co. Dublin

Shrine to Our Lady at Lady Well
Slane Castle Demesne, Co. Meath

Visitors at Lady Well
Slane

**Rags and petitions
on a laurel bush at
Saint Brigid's Well**
Faughart Upper

**Rag tree at Saint
Ciaran's Well**
Castlekeeran,
Co. Meath

Ladle at Saint Ciaran's Well
Castlekeeran, Co. Meath

'White' Well
Dowth, Co. Meath

Toberfinn
Fieldstown

Piscina at the 'Jumping Church'
Kildemock

Bullaun near Saint Patrick's Well
Kilpatrick

'Wart' Well
Kilnasaggart, Co. Armagh

Ash tree at Tobar an tSolais
Killineer

the impressions of Saint Patrick's foot, knee and staff, made as he prayed there.

The well is lined with big stones and covered with a large slab and grass. Its water bubbles up through the silt at the bottom; it is cool and clear with a very good taste. A small stream drains the well northwards to the wood.

Garrett's Well,
Hacklim Townland, Kildemock Parish

Looking for Garrett's Well will lead you to discover much more! From Blakestown Cross, south of Ardee, the road runs east to the ruins of the 'Jumping Church' at Kildemock, where Mr. Patrick Reilly ably guides people around the church and graveyard. He grew up in the area and knows every stone in it.

Follow the road from the church for about four hundred yards, then turn east into a lane which is enchanting in spring as it is covered and verged with yellow flowers. More than two centuries ago this lane was the only highway going up the hill from Ardee. Many people who lived in neighbouring cottages started their journey to America on it.

Garrett's Well is situated in a green field, on the eastern side of a horse-jump. Hidden under a small mound and sheltered by huge ash trees, it lies quite close to the lane.

The well is built of roughly shaped stones set back into the mound and covered with a flat slab. The opening is not large, but in the spring the setting sun sends its rays to the purple and grey stones at the back of the well-house. This well holds water only in wet weather.

Was this well connected with Garrett's Fort, a hill north of it? Stones lie scattered on the surface of the fort. A depression in the centre is like a legendary opening into a cave. Garrett of Hacklim is said to be asleep in the mound with his warriors, on horseback, hands ready on their swords. Only a six-fingered courageous man can draw a sword hanging beside the entrance from its scabbard and break the spell. The soldiers will then wake up, ride out and fight a last battle to free Ireland.

Sunday's Well, Kilcrony Townland, Knockbridge Parish

The 'pass' to Sunday's Well is seldom used now. It is nearly lost between the aspen and ash trees that border the old coach-road. Our guide, Peggy Martin from Ardpatrick, used to come here as a child and play at the well. In the stream below, eels were caught. She led us to the 'pass' and well through the whispering aspen, past hawthorn trees hung with rags.

The narrow path is set into a very steep bank, but the going is made easier by the many handholds provided by the trees. The well, dry in summer since a modern drainage scheme took most of its water away, is surrounded by a stone-built structure. A bent ash tree grows out of the top slabs. Old leaves and bright green hart's-tongue line the bottom of the well.

But the trees still remember to leave a gap in the 'pass'. The stones leading to the well form strong steps and the narrow earthen ledge is ready to support any visitors that Peggy Martin guides to this quiet niche.

Saint Ronan's Well,
Dromiskin

Saint Ronan, born in the late 6th century, son or grandson of Berach, a chieftain of Conaill Muirthemne, was an abbot of Dromiskin. He died of yellow jaundice in 664 A.D.

He is remembered as one of the patron saints of the parish and his feast was celebrated on 30th November.

Tobar Rónáin, the well that bears his name, is not widely known now. It was an important holy well. According to the Ordnance Survey Letters it used to be in a bog, but when this bog was cut away the spring broke out in another place. The Babes Stream flowed from the well into the Fane River.

Today, the well may be reached by taking a lane behind the grounds of the school and the Catholic church. A gate into a sometimes waterlogged field at the end of the lane gives access to the well.

Saint Ronan's Well is a round, large hollow in the ground; a wire fence tries to keep animals away. The spring is stronger at certain times of the year, but when we visited it only a little water remained under a big elder bush. Some of the water drains towards the edge of the field where it then runs away through trees and bushes.

Saint Ultan's Well,
Drumgoolan Townland, Louth Parish

Three farmers chatting on the side of the road, leaning on one bicycle, seemed to wait for us to ask about the well and how to find it.

Saint Ultan was the brother of Saint Enda, Abbot of Aran, and this rarely-visited well bearing his name is near the road west of Louth village.

A bushy island of trees set in cow pastures contains a wide, deep pool of water. Duckweed and hawthorn blossoms float on the surface. The whole area is shaped like a womb with a northern opening. The ash, hawthorn and elder trees lean protectively over the quiet pool and the small stream that meanders away from it to the south.

Has this well got a cure? 'Well,' said the farmers after some reflection, 'it always cures your thirst!'

Saint Patrick's Well, Channonrock Townland

Tobar Phádraig, north of Louth village, was visited by people along a path leading from the road at Channonrock. Nowadays, horseshoes set into the stone wall help people climb into the field.

The Byrne family at the little bridge are very helpful with information on how to reach the well. A short walk through gates and two lush fields, accompanied by many curious cattle, brings one to the well - a round, shallow pool in marshy ground, in the corner of a field, surrounded by tall trees. Many stones half-submerged in the water suggest that the well might have been more built-up in former times.

A long groove on an unusual stone is said to be the imprint of Saint Patrick's staff. A hollow stone, now hidden, provided the saint with a drink and water for shaving, the razor having been made at the forge down the road, so the story goes.

This well is said to have a cure for headaches. The stations were held here on the first Sundays in May and August.

Ladywell, Marshes Upper, Dundalk

Each year, in the middle of August, pilgrims from Dundalk and much farther afield, gather on the southern side of Dundalk, not far from the main road, where a blue gate and sign indicate the path to Ladywell, to celebrate the Patron Day there.

Patron Days or patterns often combined penitential and religious rituals with festive celebrations such as races, wrestling and other games. These latter activities often ended with people in high spirits, leading to sore heads and broken limbs. This was also the case at Ladywell.

Isaac Butler wrote in 1744 about this 'place of pilgrimage from most parts of the Kingdom' that 'the days reserved by the devotees are the 15th of August and the 8th of September', but also noted 'the water is foul, cattle going thither to drink.'

In the 18th century, as recorded in the 'Louthiana', the well had an oval enclosure with trees surrounding and sheltering it like a dome.

About a hundred years ago iron railings were erected and during the 1950s many changes were made. In 1994 the paths around the well were laid with tarmacadam and four big horse-chestnut trees mark the corners of the enclosure. The white-painted well-house in the centre looks like a tiny cottage. It has a statue of Our Lady and an arch over the steps and the low 'door'. The whole of the interior is filled with water.

It is believed that on the eve of the feast of the Assumption, on the 14th of August, at midnight, the water rises in the well and comes up the steps. Many people gather there, before the rising takes place, for the annual procession that passes through the neighbouring housing estates.

People still come in great numbers to Ladywell, maybe not any more on foot from Donegal or with the traditional pea or pebble in the shoe for penance, but to join in prayer with the other pilgrims in a reverent fashion.

The Ladywell Committee look after the well area and its upkeep in an excellent way.

Saint Brigid's Well, Faughart Upper Townland

Probably the best known well in County Louth, Saint Brigid's Well, is situated just south of the Border on Faughart Hill. The view over to the hills and mountains of Northern Ireland is beautiful. To the south the green land slopes down to the sparkling sea in Dundalk Bay. The spire of the parish church at Kilcurry is nearly hidden among the trees. Two small pieces of bone, said to be relics of Saint Brigid's cranium, rest in a reliquary in the church.

To find Faughart follow the road north out of Dundalk, turn left before the large roundabout, then follow signs to the shrine. Faughart, a location of great historical importance and site of former battles, was the birth place of Saint Brigid. The well dedicated to her is easy to spot in the ancient church site and graveyard. It has a stout, much repaired conical stone structure. Several steps lead down to the water; the well sometimes dries up in summer.

This well is often visited by people for healing purposes, especially those with eye disorders. On the large laurel bush beside the well many rags, threads, rosaries, even bits of lace and potpourri hearts hang; some petitions, written on paper, are rolled up and left in the intertwining branches. Pilgrims walk *deiseal* or sunwise around the well.

In the graveyard there are two other objects of interest; 'Saint Brigid's Pillar' may be the base of an old cross, and 'Saint Brigid's Stone' or 'Bed' is a horseshoe-shaped mound. Penitential exercises, part of the traditional stations, were performed at the ruined church, the graveyard, the well, and also the Pillar and the Stone.

From Faughart Upper a 'pass' called 'Saint Brigid's Road' leads past the Motte through fields down about half a mile to *Sruthán Bhríde* ('Saint Brigid's Stream'). Saint Brigid is said to have come down from her home to this stream. *Sruthán Bhríde* is also, even now, a much visited site, where the more modern signs of Christian devotion mix with much older objects like the stones and bullauns that are positioned along the lower part of the site. Cures are also attributed to them, threads and rosaries are hanging on the wire fence nearby. The stream is a quiet brook that bubbles up under the tall trees and then emerges into the open green space.

Saint Brigid's Day on the 1st of February, is celebrated with a triduum, a torch-lit procession and a blessing. Another procession in the afternoon of the first Sunday in July, in which the relic from the Kilcurry church is carried, starts from the church and winds its way up to the Faughart sites. In September a pilgrimage takes place in the Irish language. But the well and stream are places visited all during the year by people wishing to pray and seeking healing.

'White' Well,
Dowth, County Meath

Almost opposite the Netterville Institute a small lane leads northwards, down towards the River Mattock. Two magnificent horse chestnut trees and a big rusty gate lead on the right hand side into a field, past a ruined farmhouse, where the fireplace with an elegantly-curved lintel still stands tall. Continuing a little farther north in that field and through a gap in the hedge, one walks around the back of this well which is covered with bushes.

The whole area of the well is fenced in as cattle often graze nearby. The setting sun lights up this very peaceful spot. Mature trees shelter it.

The 'White' Well is in a big structure built of stone and red brick. The whole interior is whitewashed, but moss, ivy, hart's-tongue and the passage of time have added several shades of green to it. The clear, cool water flows through a gap in the back wall of the well into a square basin lined with big stone slabs. The water level stays the same, as the outflow under the front slab allows the water to run down towards the stream.

The tall well-house has a barrel-vaulted ceiling and on each side of the structure are stone 'seats' and 'shelves'. Was this a butter well? The interior of the well-house is very cold, the water pure and fresh, as it is running constantly. It would have been a good place to wash and maybe even store butter.

Now the seats let the visitor rest in this cool and very quiet interior and the water offers a refreshing drink.

'Verruca' Well,
Fennor, Slane, County Meath

Tom Walsh from Tullyallen told us about this 'well' and explained that it had a cure for warts: 'Touch the point of a pin on the verruca, drop the pin into the well and you will be cured of the verruca'.

Fennor is on the southern side of the bridge at Slane, where the road to Dublin winds up the hill giving a spectacular view of the Boyne River. In front of the ruined Fennor Castle is a small churchyard, still used today, that holds the collapsing stone walls of an old church. The 'Verruca' Well is in the grounds of this little cemetery.

The 'well' is not actually a spring, but possibly the base of an old cross. The cut stone has a rectangular cavity in it, which fills with rainwater.

Such 'wells' are called **bullauns** (Irish *ballán*, 'a natural cup-like hole in a rock'). They may be a natural cavity in a stone, a holy water font or a *piscina* now under the open sky in or near a ruined church. The water in such a cavity is often considered to have healing powers.

Some other **bullauns** are to be found in Dromiskin beside the old church ruin. Also in Stickillen outside the old church in the graveyard is an upright stone, maybe a former holy water stoop. At the 'Jumping Church' near Ardee are to be found *piscinae* and holy water fonts that fill up with rainwater. A big reddish-coloured rock in a field near the standing stone at Kilnasaggart, just north of the Border, sits in the grass and has a big, perfectly round, deep cavity that is always filled with water. It is called a 'wart well'.

Saint John's Well, Mornington, County Meath

It took three attempts, visits to Navan Library to consult Viscount Gormanston's beautifully-drawn map, help from local residents and their dogs, huge sheltering trees during a sudden shower, members of several families in wellington boots, to finally locate this formerly often-visited well dedicated to Saint John.

The Glen in Mornington hides a lovely walk over grassland and under trees. The forked stream meanders down the Glen, sometimes nearly hidden under masses of yellow flag irises. The area near the stream is very wet and one expects to find a well anywhere in the dense bushes or under trees.
It is possible to join the path through the Glen just south of the stone house, before the new church. A stile in the wall helps one into the meadow where an open well provides water for the cattle. Following the path towards the southwest, but before Glen House, a wide open, square-shaped field is reached, with a tall, slender standing stone in its centre, which is pierced with a small, round hole near the top. The dowsing rods indicated an underground water course through the field, exactly under the stone, leading north to the well. Mr. Joe Smith with his dogs brought us to Saint John's Well. His wife Una remembers visiting the well as a child with her father. It used to have lots of rags hanging from the nearby bushes.

The well is built into the steep bank, under very tall, mature trees. At present an opening reaching three or four feet into the bank, allows the water to come out. The basin of the well is now covered with logs and stones to protect cattle from breaking a leg, but the water flows up readily when the wood is removed. A high semi-circular stone structure shelters the well. The niche on the left side of the well might once have held a mug or a jug for drinking the water. It would have been possible to do rounds there, up and around and down the bank in this shady, very intensely green place.

Saint Columcille's Well, Calliaghstown, County Meath

The road from Julianstown to Duleek leads, almost unnoticed, past one of the most beautifully-built holy wells. The structure proudly turns its back to the road and presents its face to the sun. Lush green grass hides the outflow of the well which flows towards pink and white flowering hawthorn trees.

The strong spring fills a large circular pool, stone walls shaping it. Another stone wall, higher at the back, surrounds the site. The statue of a young king from the late 13th or early 14th century is set into the back, overlooking the well. People often think that it is Saint Columcille. A huge stone slab, set on edge at the front of the wall, completes the ring. The large opening underneath allows water to be drawn from the well. The overflow runs onto the flags, and steps invite you to take off shoes and socks, wade through the water and then walk a complete circle around the well.

Cures for warts, corns, sores and also for eye ailments, are ascribed to Saint Columcille's Well.

The Brady family who live nearby keep the waters at the well clean.

Lady Well, Slane Castle Demesne, County Meath

Every year the gate beside the 'Rock Concert Gates' into the grounds of Slane Castle is opened on the feast of the Assumption of Our Lady on the 15th of August. Parked cars, and people walking through the gates, alert one to the fact that people are visiting Lady Well, close to the River Boyne.

Many of the people have been coming regularly to this well, dedicated to Our Lady, for fifty years or more. The steep path through the grass, down to the Boyne's edge and leading along the river to the well, and then up again through the trees to reach the road, is busy with people of all ages. Whole families come. Those who have already made the visit to the well advise newcomers as to which of the paths is best on the day to reach the site of Lady Well.

The woods in that part of Slane Castle Demesne are quite dense, the Portugal laurel having grown into huge trees. Set back a little under the trees and shrubs, the spring bubbles out of the hillside through stones. The clear water spreads over the pale clay and then runs underground for a short distance to the site of the well. A rectangular opening in the ground fills with water. Flag stones allow people to step into the well and collect water to take home with them. Young boys are often given the job to fill the empty bottles. The water from the well runs under the path to join the River Boyne flowing under leafy trees.

Many of the people who visit the well say prayers by its side, reach down to wet their faces and drink the water. They also use the Portugal laurel leaves and clay together with the water for healing. These are applied to the afflicted parts of their bodies, or also taken home to be used by themselves or others.

There is a very friendly atmosphere at this well. While some people pray fervently, others chat with friends and rest before undertaking the climb back up the path to the road.

In the woods, farther along little-used avenues and paths, Saint Erc's Hermitage is found. These are ecclesiastical ruins from the late sixteenth or early seventeenth century, and have an earlier tower. The hermitage takes its name from Erc, the first bishop of Slane, consecrated by St. Patrick. Saint Erc died in 514 A.D.

Saint Mobhí's Well,
Grange Townland, near Skerries, County Dublin

A good starting point for finding this well is at the gates of Ardgillan Castle, then take the road south opposite its entrance. The well is in a narrow strip of woodland. Nearby are the ruins of a 14th century church, and an old graveyard still in use today.

Once you step off the road and through a rusty gate into the dense wood which envelops you, the wind and the birds move in the branches of the tall trees, and the dappled sunlight plays on the ground. After a while the path is blocked by a huge ash tree growing over the well, like a sentinel. The path divides to allow for the well in the centre, then unites again and continues through the wood.

The water, running underground at right angles to the path, keeps the well at a constant level. Stone flags lead down to it and moss covers many of the huge stones that line both sides of the steps. The well-water is cool and clear. A round basin-stone close to the well is always filled with rain water.

Local people used to visit Saint Mobhí's Well in order to make their petitions, especially before examinations. They circled the well three times, picked a leaf from the tree, dipped it in the well and then left it in the bullaun stone. The well is also said to cure toothache, headache and sore throat.

The bark of the tall ash tree is covered with markings and initials. The enormous stones that form the well-house seem to have been there from the very distant past. Some bear cup marks, lines and more recent crosses. One of the stones is said to have been flung there by Fionn MacCumhaill as the marks on it look like the imprints of gigantic fingers.

One can sense the past by touching these old rocks, and observe the way the ash tree protects this beautiful well.

Saint Brigid's Well, Tobersool, County Dublin

Past Gormanston College and Castle a small road leads south across a humpback bridge over the river Delvin. Soon afterwards a small road turns west. A lane leading south marks the corner field where the well is situated on Mr. Joseph Dunne's land.

The small opening in the northern hedge of the cornfield allows people to slip in without disturbing the farmer. Not far from this hedge is Saint Brigid's Well. Tall holly trees and other prickly vegetation guard the well and keep all but the most determined visitor at a distance from the water.

The well, almost in the centre of the encircling trees and bushes, is rectangular in shape. Big flags and some round stones form the four sides.

Tobersool was full in February, on the saint's feast day. Recent wet weather had flooded the well-site and left a fine coating of dust on the low slabs and the ivy. In dry weather the water in the well sinks much lower.

The well is reputed to cure sore eyes and has given its name to the area around it: *Tobar súl* ('Well of the Eyes').

Some Drogheda Wells

Roches Well, Moneymore

Roches Well, named after a family who used to farm in the area, is near the Moneymore Housing Estate at the edge of a field. The well is under trees and bushes festooned with ivy. A shape like an enormous horseshoe built from stone and concrete keeps the well clean, but the plentiful water spills out onto the surrounding area.

According to a resident in the old cottage nearby, the quality of the water is very good and it is used for drinking and tea-making.

Ben Kelly-Moloney and some of his young friends love to visit 'their' well, an enchanted place so near their home.

Newfoundwell

According to legend a woman washed clothes in the original well and thus polluted it. The well dried up, but rose again as a spring in a field south of the road near the railway bridge. This explains the name; 'New-found-well'. The old well, called 'Blind Well', is to be seen in the wall of the present-day 'Bridgeford Leisure Centre'. A second explanation given for the well moving to another site is that the original well was disturbed when the railway was built. A third well was down in the nearby glen.

Saint Patrick's Well,
Patrickswell Lane

The area west of Patrickswell Lane contains several wells and springs.

The well which gave its name to the lane, is thought to be under the floor of the former Robinson's Auction Rooms. About twelve years ago Jim Garry and Larry Conlon saw the well after a carpet had been rolled back, and a cover removed. It was a circular well, very deep and it was sometimes troublesome because of flooding. The well is named after Saint Patrick, who is said to have used it when he visited Drogheda.

Another well is to be found close to Saint Mary d'Urso Abbey. When the new Garda Station was being built a well gave a lot of trouble to the builders.

Saint Patrick's Well,
The Dale

This well was covered over by Drogheda Corporation. A plaque was put up on which there were handles, taps and a metal cup to enable people to draw water. This plaque is now preserved in the Millmount Museum, thanks to the late Harry Fairclough. On the plaque is written; 'Corporation of Drogheda 1860, Patk. Byrne Esqr, Mayor' and displays the Star and Crescent in the four corners.

Dyer Street

Possibly the loveliest well in Drogheda could be seen for a few short weeks only, when in 1996 excavations were carried out north of Dyer Street. The foundations of the old houses could be observed clearly. In one of the houses a circular well, about one metre in diameter, built of stones, was found. The well dates back to the 12th century. In later times its enclosing structure was raised higher with mortared stone to allow for subsequent floor levels. This well flooded once or twice a month, probably due to high tides, but for the rest of the time the water was fresh.

Saint John's Well, Ballsgrove

It was, or is, situated on the slope of the hill below Highfield, south-west of the Bus Station. The well is remembered by some local people, but it has not been located recently, as some areas are impossible to investigate.

Fairywell

On the Donore Road, the Fairywell Tyre Centre recalls with its name the well that used to be at the bottom of the slope from the Watery Hill, behind the Tyre Centre. Its waters are now carried underground through the premises to a manhole.

Greenbatter

East of the former flax mill, now 'Porterhouse Ltd.,' in the grounds of the Garden Centre, was a well that supplied the area. A pump house was built over it later. Now the well and pump station are under the small shop of the Garden Centre.

Stockwell Street

This street bears the name of a well used to provide water for cattle.

North Quay

The water from this well flows out of the Quay wall, opposite house No. 5 on the Quay.

Many houses, shops and pubs had their own wells. Some, in the lower lying areas, used to flood periodically. One man told us that he visited a pub where strange noises could be heard under the floor. When the publican descended into the cellar he stepped right into the water and was surrounded by floating bottles.

During the First World War, at a time when water was very scarce, a well in the premises of a public house kept the centre of Drogheda supplied with water.

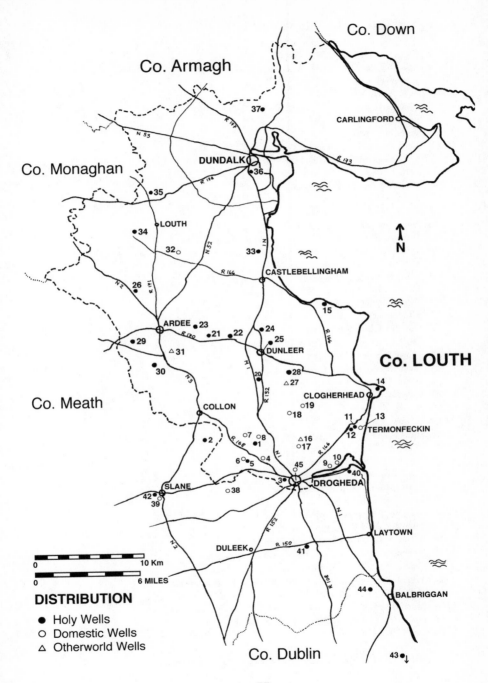

Co. Down

Co. Armagh

Co. Monaghan

Co. Meath

Co. LOUTH

Co. Dublin

37●

CARLINGFORD ○

●35

●34   ●LOUTH

32○

DUNDALK ○
●36

33●

CASTLEBELLINGHAM ○

15

26●

ARDEE ⊕ ●23

●29   21● 22●

△31

30●

COLLON

●2

○7 ○8
●1

6○●5 ●4

42●
39○

SLANE ●

○38

●24
25
DUNLEER ○

●28
△27

20●

CLOGHERHEAD ○

○19
○18

△16
○17

45
3● DROGHEDA

14

11   13
○○ TERMONFECKIN
12

9 10
○○
● ●40

LAYTOWN ○

DULEEK ○   41●

R 150

44●   ○ BALBRIGGAN

43●↓

N

0 ———————— 10 Km
0 ———————— 6 MILES

DISTRIBUTION

● Holy Wells
○ Domestic Wells
△ Otherworld Wells

DISTRIBUTION OF WELLS VISITED IN 1996

1 Tobar an tSolais, Killineer
2 Saint Columcille's Well, Glasallen, County Meath
3 Toberboice Well, Mell
4 Sally Well, Mell
5 Saint Brigid's Well, Tullyallen
6 Some Wells in the Tullyallen Area
7 Wells in Coolfore
8 Wells under Red Mountain
9 Wells in the Woods of Beaulieu House
10 Splink Well, near Baltray
11 Saint Feichín's Well, Termonfeckin
12 Trinity Well, Termonfeckin
13 Castle Well, Termonfeckin
14 Saint Dennis's Well, Clogher
15 Toberhullamog, Saint Colman's Well, Salterstown
16 Tobershowney, Carntown
17 Well at Listoke, Commons
18 Toberfinn, Fieldstown
19 The 'Comfortable' Well, Brownstown
20 Tober Maura, Mullary
21 Saint Mairéad's Well, Toberdoney House
22 Saint Finian's Well, Dromin
23 Saint Patrick's Well, Stickallen
24 Tobar Mhuire, Cappoge
25 Saint Brigid's Well, Dunleer
26 Tobar Mhichíl, Charlestown
27 Toberanelshy, Gallstown
28 Spa Well, Marley
29 Toberdoney, Shanlis
30 Saint Patrick's Well, Kilpatrick
31 Garrett's Well, Hacklim
32 Sunday's Well, Kilcrony
33 Saint Ronan's Well, Dromiskin
34 Saint Ultan's Well, Drumgoolan
35 Saint Patrick's Well, Channonrock
36 Ladywell, Marshes Upper, Dundalk
37 Saint Brigid's Well, Faughart Upper
38 'White' Well, Dowth, County Meath
39 'Verruca' Well, Fennor, Slane, County Meath
40 Saint John's Well, Mornington, County Meath
41 Saint Columcille's Well, Calliaghstown, County Meath
42 Lady Well, Slane Castle Demesne, County Meath
43 Saint Mobhí's Well, Grange, near Skerries, County Dublin
44 Saint Brigid's Well, Tobersool, County Dublin
45 Some Drogheda Wells

All wells visited are in County Louth unless stated otherwise.

Glossary

boreen, *bóithrín:*	country lane
bullaun, *ballán:*	a rock with cup-shaped holes, often said to be the imprints of body parts of a saint
cup marks:	natural or man-made cup-shaped holes in a large stone
deiseal:	walking in a right-handed, clockwise direction, the direction of the sun
doing the rounds:	performing certain penitential exercises or saying prayers while walking around the well or other places
domestic well:	water is drawn from it for domestic purposes
dowsing rod:	one forked branch or two L-shaped metal rods used by dowsers to divine water, etc.
'dress' the well:	to decorate the well on Pattern Days with flowers, leafy branches, ribbons, candles, etc.
duckweed:	(*Lemna minor*), a tiny floating plant covering still water, often growing like a green carpet
hart's tongue:	(*Phillitis scolpendrium vulgare*), a fern, 'lingua cervi', so named from the shape of the narrow, undivided fronds
holy well:	a well or spring reputed to have miraculuous healing properties
offerings at wells:	coins, shells, stones, etc. left in or beside a well
pass:	a path or opening leading to a well or church
pattern, patron, *patrún:*	festivities connected with Patron Saint's Day or the patron of a well
petitions:	supplication or prayer, sometimes written on paper or ribbons and left in trees or the stonework of a well
penal times:	penal legislation against Catholics, 1695-1709
piscina:	a stone basin with a drain for the water used in ceremonial ablutions, often found in chuch ruins
pond skater:	an insect of the family *Gerridea*, which has the ability to skim across the surface of the water
rags, strings, ribbons, garters, pins, rosaries:	objects left at a well, usually hanging on trees or bushes, symbolising ailments or problems
service tree:	*sorbus*
spa well:	a well containing certain minerals

srath:	low lying land beside a river
standing stone:	megalithic upright stone
stations:	prayers, religious exercises, penances or ceremonies performed at certain locations
stop:	stone-stop, a large stone placed at the front to retain the water in the well
tobar:	Irish for well; anglicised Tober, Tubber
Toberdoney:	*Tobar Domhnaigh*, Sunday's Well, people gathered there after Sunday Mass, to exchange greetings or drink the water
triduum:	a ceremony taking place on three days
water rising:	the water in some wells is said to rise at certain times and is then thought to be especially potent

Bibliography

Buckley, Victor M. & Sweetman, David P.	*Archaeological Survey of County Louth* (Dublin 1991)
Carroll, Cathleen	'Termonfeckin in the 1920s and 30s', in *Down All Those Years and More* (Termonfeckin, 1988)
Cartin, Joseph	*An Essay on Patriotism; Together with Legends and Stories of Louth* ... (Drogheda, 1839)
Conlon, Larry	'Holy Wells of Mid-Louth', in *The Local News*, 1986-87
Connolly, Susan	*For the Stranger*, Dublin, 1993
Crilly, Anne	'Some Drogheda Wells', *Journal of the Old Drogheda Society*, (1976), 10-12
D'Alton, John	*History of Drogheda*, (1844)
Deane, J.	'Extracts from Isaac Butler's Journal', *County Louth Archaeological and Historical Journal*, v. 2 (1922), 93-108
Garry, James	*The Streets and Lanes of Drogheda* (Drogheda, 1996)
Garstin, John R. (ed.)	'Louth Ordnance Survey Letters', *County Louth Archaeological and Historical Journals:* 'Beaulieu', iv, 1, (1916), 103 'Cappoge', v, 4, (1924), 282 'Channonrock', vi, 1, (1925), 41 'Charlestown', v, 3, (1923), 202 'Clogher', iv, 4, (1919-20), 333 'Dromin', v, 3, (1923), 200 'Dromiskin', vi, 1, (1925), 46 'Drumgoolan', vi, 1, (1925), 41 'Dundalk', vii, 1, (1929), 64 'Dunleer', v, 1, (1921), 33 'Faughart Upper', vii, 1, (1929), 63-64

'Hacklim', vii, 1, (1929), 54
'Kilcrony', vi, 1, (1925), 42
'Killineer', iv, 1, (1916), 100
'Kilpatrick', vii, 1, (1929), 53-58
'Marlestown', iv, 4, (1919-20), 337
'Mullary', v, 3, (1923), 205
'Salterstown', v, 1, (1921), 30
'Shanlis', vi, 3, (1927), 129
'Stickillen', v, 3, (1923), 198
'Termonfeckin', iv, 4, (1919-20), 335

A History of Julianstown (Irish Countrywomen's, Association, Julianstown, 1982)

Jones, Francis   *The Holy Wells of Wales*, (Cardiff, 1922)

King, Philip   *Monasterboice Heritage*, (Monasterboice, 1994)

'Ladywell Shrine'   leaflet issued by Ladywell Shrine Committee, Dundalk.

'Ladywell Shrine - Dundalk's Own Place of Pilgrimage',
    Dundalk Democrat, 10th August, 1996.

Leslie, Rev. James B.   *History of Kilsaran*, (Dundalk, 1908)

Logan, Patrick   *The Holy Wells of Ireland*, (Gerrards Cross, 1980)

Lysaght, Patricia   'Trees in Irish Folk Tradition', *Irish Biological Records Centre* (Dublin, 1979)

MacIomhair,
Rev. Diarmuid   *Fochart*
(Dundalk, n.d.)

Moody, T.W. &
Martin, F.X.   *The Course of Irish History*
(Dublin, 1984)

Moore, Michael J.   *Archaeological Inventory of County Meath*
(Dublin, 1987)

Murphy, Donald	'A Brief History of the Parish to 1900 A.D.', in *Down All Those Years and More*, (Termonfeckin 1988), 13-29
Murphy, Michael J.	*Tyrone Folk Quest*, (Belfast, 1973)
O'Connor, Lil,	'Faughart Investigations', *County Louth Archaeological and Historical Journal*, xvi, 2, (1966), 125
Ó Danachair, C.	'Holy Well Legends in Ireland', *Saga och Sed*, (1959), 35-43
Ó Danachair, C.	The Holy Wells of Co. Limerick', *Journal of the Royal Society of Antiquaries of Ireland*, vol.85, Part 2, (1955), 193-217
Ó Danachair, C.	'The Holy Wells of Co. Dublin', *Reportorium Novum*, vol. 2, No. 1 (1958-59), 68-87

Official Guide to Louth and Meath (Dublin, n.d.)

O'Neill, C.P.	*History of Dromiskin*, (Dundalk, 1984)
Robinson, Aidan P.	*Ancient Drogheda*, (Swords, 1994)
Saint-Exupéry, A. de	*The Little Prince*, translation © Katherine Woods, 1945, (London, 1974)

Schools' Manuscripts' Collection 1937-38, Dept. of Irish Folklore, University College, Dublin

Stubbs, Major General F.W.	'Holy Wells in County Louth' and 'Wells Bearing Irish Names', *Archaeological and Historical Journal*, ii, 1, (1908), 40

Togher Through the Years (Irish Countrywomen's Association, Togher, 1993)

'Townland Surveys of County Louth', *County Louth Archaeological and Historical Journals*:
   'Beaulieu' xix, 4, (1980), 274; James Garry
   'Callystown', vii, 2, (1930), 182-86; Rev. J.G.
          MacCooey

'Charlestown', xxi, 3, (1987), 311; Ann Flynn
'Faughart Lower', xvi, 2, (1966), 121; Rev. D.
MacIvor
'Faughart Upper', xvi, 2, (1966), 111; Rev. D.
MacIvor
'Hacklim', xii, 2, (1950), 125-27; Rev. D. MacIvor
'Kildemock Miscellanea', xiii, 4, (1956), 412, 415;
Rev. D. MacIvor
'Kilpatrick', x, 4, (1944), 327; xii, 1 (1949), 30
Rev. D. McIvor
'Mell', xxii, 2, (1990), 150; James Garry
'Navan', xvii, 3, (1971), 169-170; Rev. D. MacIvor
'Paughanstown', xii, 2, (1950), 117; Rev. D.
MacIvor
'Stickillen', xiii, 4, (1956), 399; Rev. D. MacIvor
'Termonfeckin', xxi, 4, (1988), 398; Donald Murphy

Trench, C.E.F.   *Slane* (Slane, 1987)

Tuite, Breeda   'Local Folklore', *Mellifont Parish Magazine*, 1979

Wilde, William R.   *The Beauties of the Boyne and its Tributary, the Blackwater* (2nd ed., Dublin, 1850)

Wright, Thomas,   *Louthiana* (London, 1748)

Maps

Ordnance Survey County Meath, 1837, Viscount Gormanston, Navan Library.

Ordnance Survey Maps of Ireland; County Louth, 1835 to present day, Drogheda Library.

Ordnance Survey of Ireland; County Meath, Navan Library.

Ordnance Survey of Ireland; Maps of Drogheda 1861-1870, 1:500, Drogheda Library.

Acknowledgments

Many people have helped in the preparation of this book. Thanks to Alison Kelly for her many good ideas and for proof-reading the manuscript.

Many thanks to Michael Holohan for assistance with sponsorship and for proof-reading.

The authors wish to thank Dr. Patricia Lysaght for writing the Foreword to the book. She is also Irish language editor of this book.

Anne-Marie Moroney would like to thank Larry Conlon for his kind help in locating many of the wells mentioned in this book.

She is also most grateful to Father Edwin Flynn OFM Cap. for his help with the computer.

Susan Connolly would like to acknowledge the support of *Dúchas* (Drogheda Oral Heritage Project) which enabled this project to commence, and of *Glór na nGael* which ensured its completion.

She would also like to thank Lia Mills, Liz MacArdle, Paddy Dillon and Patricia Lysaght for reading drafts of the poems.

We are grateful to Judith Hoad who gave us much useful advice for the publication of this work.

Thanks to the staff of Drogheda and Navan Libraries for their assistance.

The writing of this book would not have been possible without the help of many people encountered in 1996. They talked about the wells in their vicinity and guided us to those wells. We take this opportunity to thank them for their willingness to share their knowledge of this aspect of our heritage with us.

Sponsors

Archaeological Consultancy Services
Barbican Literary Group
Bank of Ireland
Becton Dickinson
Boann (Drogheda Women Artists Group)
Martin Butterly & Co. Limited
Mrs. Sheila Callan
Malachy Callan
Coca-Cola Atlantic
Dr. Mary Connolly
Stephen Connolly
Drogheda Credit Union
Droichead Arts Centre
Dunne Water Services, Dromiskin
Fyffes Limited, Dundalk
The Heritage Council of Ireland
Michael Holohan
Louth Archaeological and Historical Society
Mellifont Credit Union
Mrs. Eileen Murphy
Lia Mills and Simon Robinson
O'Grady's Gardens, Coolfore
Old Drogheda Society
Porterhouse Limited
Premier Periclase
Úna Sheehan

INDEX

ague,46
Annagassan,46
Ardee,50,51,52,55,59,67
Ardgillan Castle,71
Ardpatrick,60
ash tree,3,33,42,49,50,59,60,62,71,72
aspen,60
Assumption of Our Lady,1,53,63,69
asthma,58
Atlantis,3

Babes Stream,61
backache,35
Balgatheran Townland,33
ballán,67
Ballymakenny Road,47
Ballywater river, stream,42,43
Baltray,42
bare feet,2,35
Barnattin,33,41
basin-stone,71
Beaulieu House,3,41,42
Beaulieu Townland,41,42
Begrath,40
Berach,61
Blakestown Cross,59
Blessed Virgin, the,53
Boylan Family,58
Boyne Estuary,42
Brady Family,69
broken limbs,35,63
Brownstown,48,49
bullaun,58,65,67,71
Butler, Isaac,34,63
butter well,66

'Comfortable' Well, the,49
Cains Well,37
Conaill Muirthemne,61
candles,2,33,35,46,49,50,55
Cappoge,18,53
Carney's lane,41
Carntown Townland,3,47
carry water home in bottles,1,35,53,70
Castle Well,44
chalybeate well,36
Channonrock Townland,62
Charlestown Townland,55
Church of Ireland,49,55
clay,70
Clogher Townland,15,44
Clogherhead,44,45
Collon,2,34
Commons Townland,47
Cooldrumman,51
Cooley Mountains,45
Cooley Peninsula,46
Coolfore,40
County Louth Archaeological Journal,54
County Louth Ordnance Survey Letters,43,61
Culfionn,48
Cunningham's house,34
cup marks,58,67,72

cure for corns,69
cure for eye diseases,2,34,35,38,46,54,65,69,72
cure for sore throat,71
cure for sores,69
cure for toothache,71
cure for verrucas,67
cure for warts,67,69

D'Alton,40
Dawes Well,37
deiseal,2,65
do rounds,2,35,51,53,65,68
Doagh stream,34
Donore Road,75
dowsing rod,36,68
Dowth,66
'dress' the well,2,35,44
drink the water,35,37,38,42,44,48,53,55,58,62,66,70
Drogheda,3,36,40,41,47,73,74,76
Drogheda Bus Station,75
Drogheda Wells,3,73
Dromin,50,51
Dromiskin,61,67
Drumgoolan Townland,61
Drummond Delap, William, Esq.,40
duckweed,43,62
Duleek, County Meath,69
Dundalk,63,64
Dundalk Bay,45,64
Dunleer,49,51,54,56
Dunleer Parish,53,54
Dunleer Quarry,56
Dunleer Townland,54
Dyer Street,3,74

elder bush,61,62
emigration,52,59
Erc,70,71
examinations,71
excavations,74
'Eye' Well,72

'fairy well',55
Fane River,66
Faughart Hill,2,64,65
Faughart Upper Townland,64,65
flag irises,51,58,68
feast of the Assumption, 15th August,1,2,53,63,69
Fennor,67
festive celebrations,63
Fethis,44
Fieldstown Townland,48
Fionn MacCumhaill,48,72
First World War,76
flooding wells,74,75,76
Flynn's river,48

Gallstown House,56
Gallstown Townland,3,19,55
games,35,50,63
Garrett of Hacklim,60
Garrett's Fort,4,60
Garrett's Well,4,20,59
garters,35

Gearóid Iarla,4
Glasallen Townland,34
Glen House,68
Glen, the, Mornington, County Meath,68
Gormanston College and Castle,72
Grange Townland, County Dublin,71
Grangebellew,56
Greenbatter,75

Hacklim Townland,20,59
Harestown Road,49
hart's-tongue,41,42,58,60,66
hawthorn tree,3,33,41,60,62,69
headaches,62,71
healing,35,50,56,64,65,67,70
hedge school,51
Highfield,75
Himalayan Balsam,43
Hurcle Hill,34
Hurcle Road,34,36

I.C.A. College, An Grianán,43
initials and crosses,45,71
inscription,50
Iona,51

Julianstown, County Meath,69
Jumping Church,59,67

McKeever Family,57
Marlestown Civil Parish,56
Marley Townland,3,25,56
Marshes Upper Townland,63
Mass, after,38,48
Mattock river,66
May morning,3,47
Mell,36,37

Kilcrony Townland,22,60
Kilcurry,64,65
Kildemock Parish,58,59
Killian's House,52
Killineer,30,33
Killineer Townland,33,41
Kilnasaggart,67
Kilpatrick Townland,58
King William's Glen,38
Knights Templars and Hospitallers,49
Knockbridge Parish,60

Lady Day,28
Lady Well, Slane, County Meath,1,27,69,70
Ladywell Committee,64
Ladywell, Marshes Upper, Dundalk,2,63
laurel bush,2,65
leaf,70,71
ledge,49,66
Linn Duachill monastery,46
Listoke, well at,3,47
Lord Rokeby,56
Louth Parish,61
Louth village,62
Louthiana,63
luck,47

Mellifont,33,34,40
Millmount Museum,74
minerals,57
Moneymore Housing Estate,73
Mornington, County Meath,68
moving well,33,58
mug,35,44,48,68
Muire na nGael,2
Mullary,16,49

Navan Townland,3
Newfoundwell,73
niche,68
North Quay,76

old coach-road,60
Oldbridge,39,40
otherworld,3
Our Lady,2,69

Pan Well,43
'pass',39,60,65
Patrickswell Lane,74
Patron,2,34,50,55,61,63
Patron Day,2,50,63
Pattern,2,34,35,44,45,46,47,50,63
pattern day,1,35
pea or pebble in the shoe,64
Penal times,40
penance,64
penitential exercises,63,65
petitions,45,65,71
pilgrimage,34,35,54,63,65
pin,67
Piperstown Townland,48
piscina,67
plaque,48,74
polluting the well,33,58,73
pond skater,47
Portugal laurel,70
pray for a return to Ireland,52
procession,46,64,65

Queensborough,42

races,63
rags,2,35,50,58,60,65
Red Mountain,41
relics,64,65
religious rituals,63
reported cures,38,46
ribbons,35
Richardstown Castle,52
River Boyne,1,37,41,67,70
River Delvin,72
Roches Well, Moneymore,73
Rokeby Hall,56
rosary,2,35,53,58,65

sailor cured,45
Saint Brigid,2,54,64,65,72
Saint Brigid's cranium,64
Saint Brigid's Day, 1st February,65,72
'Saint Brigid's Road',65

'Saint Brigid's Stream',65
Saint Brigid's Well, Tullyallen,38
Saint Brigid's Well, Dunleer,54
Saint Brigid's Well, Faughart,2,64
Saint Brigid's Well, Marley Townland,56,57
Saint Brigid's Well, Stickillen,53
Saint Brigid's Well, Tobersool, County Dublin,72
Saint Buithe,36,37
Saint Colman's Well,46
Saint Columcille,51,69
Saint Columcille's Well, Glasallen, County Meath,2,34,35
Saint Columcille's Well, Calliaghstown, County Meath,69
Saint Dennis's Gale,45
Saint Dennis's Well,15,44,45
Saint Erc's Hermitage,70
Saint Feichín's Well,17,42
Saint Feichín's monastery,42
Saint Finian of Movilla,51,52
Saint Finian's Psalter,51
Saint Finian's Well,51,52
Saint John's Well, Ballsgrove,75
Saint John's Well, Mornington, County Meath,68
Saint Mairéad's Well,29,50
Saint Mary d'Urso Abbey,74
Saint Michael the Archangel,55
Saint Mobhí's Well,24,71
Saint Patrick's Well, Stickillen,2,52
Saint Patrick's Well, Channonrock,62
Saint Patrick's Well, Kilpatrick,58
Saint Patrick's Well, the Dale,74
Saint Patrick's Well, Patrickswell Lane,74
Saint Ronan's Well,61
Saint Ultan,62
Saint Ultan's Well,61
Sally Well,37
Saltertown,14,46
Sarsfield, John,46
sawmill,39
Seapoint,42
service tree,57
Shanlis House,57
Shanlis Townland,21,57
Sheela's Monday,45
six-fingered man,60
Skerries, County Dublin,24,71
skin ailments,56
Slane,27,40,69
Slane Castle Demesne, County Meath,1,28,69,70
Sloan, Paddy,33
sore heads,63
Spa Well,3,25,56,57
Spa Wood,56
Splink Well,42
Sruthán Bhríde,65
stations,43,57,62,65
Stickillen Townland,2,52,67
Stockwell Street,75
stomach ailments,55
stone-stop,42,50
string,2,35,55
Sunday's Well,38,50,51,57,60
Sunday's Well, Kilcrony Townland,22,60
sunwise,2,65

taking water home,35,48,53,70
tearmann,42
Termonfeckin,17,42,43,44
'The Lord's Well',50
The Stillness of Trees,29
three farmers,61
Tigh Chillín,52
Tobar an ailsigh,56
Tobar an tSolais,30,33,38
Tobar Bhríde,57
Tobar Cholmóig,46
Tobar Domhnaigh,38,50,51,57
Tobar Feichín,43
Tobar Mháire,16,49
Tobar Mhichíl,55
Tobar Mhuire, Cappoge,18,53
Tobar na gCorr,3
Tobar na Splince,42
Tobar Phádraig, Stickillen,52,53
Tobar Phádraig, Channonrock,62
Tobar Rónáin,61
Tobar súl,72
Tobar Teorann,56
Toberanelshy,3,19,55,56
Toberboice,36,37
Tobercro,6
Toberdoney,29,50,51,57
Toberdoney House,50,51
Toberdoney Townland,50
Toberdoney, Shanlis,21,57
Toberfinn,48
Toberhullamog,14,46
Tober Maura,49
Tobershowney,3,47
Tobersool, County Dublin,72
Tobertheorin,56
Togher,46
Townley Hall,39
Townley Hall Road,39
Trinity Sunday,44
Trinity Well, Termonfeckin,43
Tullyallen,38,39
Tyrrell, Jackie,42

verruca,67
'Verruca' Well,67
Viscount Gormanston,68

wart well,67
water rising,53,64
water turning to blood,54
Well Fever,11
Well keepers,33,37,39,42,46,48,51,53,58,60,
            62,64,69,72
Well of the Light,33
White River, Dunleer,54
'White' Well, Dowth, County Meath,66
woman washing clothes,73
wrestling,63

Susan Connolly was born and lives in Drogheda, county Louth. Her poetry has appeared in journals throughout Ireland and the U.K. She had a selection of her poems published by Dedalus in **Introductions, 1989**. She is co-author of **How High the Moon** (Poetry Ireland/Co-Operation North, 1991). Her first full collection **For the Stranger** was published by Dedalus Press in 1993.

Anne-Marie Moroney was born and educated in St. Gallen, Switzerland. She has taught in Europe and Africa. In 1974 she joined her husband in Ireland and has since lived in rural County Louth, where she works as a fibre artist and a language teacher. Her articles on various topics have been published in Europe, America and New Zealand.